Skillet Co

Delicious Skillet Recipes That Will WOW
your Whole Family

BY

Stephanie Sharp

WWWWWWWWWWWWWWWWWWWWWWWWWWWWWWWW

License Notes

wwwwwwwwwwwwwwwwwwwwwwwwwwwwwwwwwwwwwwww

My deepest thanks for buying my book! Now that you have made this investment in time and money, you are now eligible for free e-books on a weekly basis! Once you subscribe by filling in the box below with your email address, you will start to receive free and discounted book offers for unique and informative books. There is nothing more to do! A reminder email will be sent to you a few days before the promotion expires so you will never have to worry about missing out on this amazing deal. Enter your email address below to get started. Thanks again for your purchase!

Just visit the link or scan QR-code to get started!

https://stephanie-sharp.subscribemenow.com

wwwwwwwwwwwwwwwwwwwwwwwwwwwwwwwwwwwww

Table of Contents

Introduction

Congratulations to you on the purchase of your cast iron skillet! Owing to its versatility, cast iron cookware is a great option. Instead of using more than one pots and pans all could be cooked in this one piece of cookware. Cast iron can be easily used on top of the stove for sautéing, stir-frying and soups, it can also be used in the oven. The use of cast iron for Paleo is very helpful since your veggies and proteins can all be cooked from the stovetop to the oven, in one dish.

Snuggling up to a cozy bowl of soup or a luscious casserole on a cool winter's eve is just one of those magical things that make the chilly weather a welcome visitor. Not only are these kinds of comfort dishes delicious, they are also supremely easy to make thanks to the magic of cast iron cookware.

The cast iron cooks evenly and is a breeze to clean, even when the meal is a messy recipe.

Although cast iron cookware has been around for centuries, its popularity has made a resurgence as more and more cooks of the new era are embracing the comfort of this established cookware and integrating it into their lives.

With our busy lives, the beauty of a one-pot dish designed to keep everyone happy is a welcome reprieve for any cook. They are sure to be a hit even with the pickiest of eaters, and only you need to know how easy it was. They never have to know your secret!

Happy cooking!

wwwwwwwwwwwwwwwwwwwwwwwwwwwwwwwwwwwwwww

Tri Colored Stuffed Pepper Casserole

Have fun trying different colors of pepper to make this meal.
A very tasty dinner dish.

Serves: 4

Total Prep Time: 40 minutes

Ingredients:

- 1-pound ground beef
- 2 tablespoons olive oil
- 3 cloves garlic (crushed and minced)
- 1 cup red bell pepper (diced)
- 1 cup yellow bell pepper (diced)
- 1 cup green bell pepper (diced)
- ½ cup red onion (diced)
- ¼ cup fresh basil (chopped)
- ¼ cup parsley (chopped)
- 1 15-ounce can crush tomatoes (with liquid)
- 1 cup tomato sauce
- 2 cups beef stock
- 1 tablespoon Worcestershire sauce
- 1 cup uncooked rice
- 1 teaspoon salt
- 1 teaspoon black pepper
- 1 cup provolone cheese (shredded)
- ½ cup parmesan cheese (freshly grated)

Directions:

Prepare a 10 or 12-inch skillet and add the olive oil over medium heat.

Cook the ground beef until browned and drain any fat.

Add the garlic, red bell pepper, yellow bell pepper, green bell pepper, and red onion. Sauté for 3-5 minutes.

Season with basil and parsley. Add the tomato sauce, beef stock and Worcestershire sauce. Stir, increase heat to medium high and bring to a boil.

Add the rice, salt, and black pepper. Stir, reduce heat and cover. Simmer for 15-20 minutes, or until rice is tender.

Sprinkle the cheese over the rice, cover and cook an additional 5 minutes, or until cheese is melted.

wwwwwwwwwwwwwwwwwwwwwwwwwwwwwwwwwwwwwwww

Breezy Brunch Skillet

Breezy Brunch Skillet might just be the main course you are waiting for. This one-pan brunch skillet will make clean-up a breeze.

Serves: 6

Total Prep Time: 45 minutes

Ingredients:

- 6 cups of frozen hash browns
- 6 eggs
- 6 slices of bacon
- 1 green pepper
- ½ cup of onion (chopped)
- ½ cup of cheddar cheese (shredded)
- ¼ teaspoon of pepper
- 1 teaspoon of salt

Directions:

Place a 10-skillet onto the stove and set the temperature to medium.

Chop the bacon and place it into the skillet.

Cook the bacon until it is crispy, roughly 5 to 10 minutes.

Drain the bacon, but reserve 2 tablespoons of the bacon grease. You can dispose of the rest.

Set aside the bacon and return the skillet to the stove without washing it. You want the flavor of the bacon that will still be in the pan.

Add the bacon grease.

Wash and seed the green pepper. Chop it.

Wash, peel, and chop the onion.

Pour the potatoes into the skillet.

Add in the green pepper and onion. Stir until the vegetables are well blended.

Season with the salt and pepper and cook for about 2 minutes.

Stir the ingredients, cover the skillet with a lid.

Cook the vegetables until the hash browns are golden brown, roughly 15 minutes. Make sure that you stir the hash browns every few minutes to prevent burning, but don't over stir them or the mixture will get mushy.

Once the hash browns are tender, use the back of a wooden spoon to create an indent into the potato. Make 4 indents, one for two eggs.

Carefully break an egg into each indentation.

Cover the skillet with the lid again and continue to cook on medium heat until the eggs have the proper consistency, roughly 8 to 10 minutes.

Shred the cheese and toss it with the bacon.

When the eggs are cooked to the desired consistency, remove the skillet from the stove.

Sprinkle the dish with cheese and bacon, cover for a minute to allow the cheese to melt slightly, then serve warm.

wwwwwwwwwwwwwwwwwwwwwwwwwwwwwwwwwwwww

Sage Roasted Chicken with Rustic Vegetables

Seasoned and well flavored to the bone. If you are having friends over, this is a perfect dish for you.

Serves: 4

Total Prep Time: 1 hour

Ingredients:

- 4 bone-in chicken breasts
- ½ cup olive oil
- 2 cups red potatoes (halved)
- 2 cups whole mini portabella mushrooms
- 1 cup red onion (cut into thick slices)
- 4 cloves garlic (crushed and minced)
- ½ cup chicken stock
- 1 tablespoon lemon juice
- 1 tablespoon whole sage leaves
- 1 teaspoon salt
- 1 teaspoon ground black peppercorns
- 1 lemon sliced

Directions:

Preheat oven to 400°F.

Prepare a 12-inch skillet and heat olive oil over medium.

Add the chicken and cook on one side for 3 minutes. Turn the chicken and add the red potatoes, portabella mushrooms, red onion, and garlic. Continue cooking for 5-7 minutes, or until chicken is browned on the outside.

Add the chicken stock, lemon juice, whole sage, salt, and ground peppercorns. Toss lightly to mix. Place the lemon slices over the chicken and vegetables.

Place in the oven and bake for 40 minutes, or until chicken is cooked through and juices run clear.

wwwwwwwwwwwwwwwwwwwwwwwwwwwwwwwwwwwwwwww

Italian Beef and Tomatoes

Here is to a hearty Italian Beef stew for dinner tonight.

Serves: 4

Total Prep Time: 35 minutes

Ingredients:

- 2 pounds choice beef steak (approximately 1½ inch in thickness)
- ¼ cup olive oil (divided)
- 5 cloves garlic (crushed and minced)
- 4 cups mini tomatoes of various colors (halved)
- 3 cups fresh spinach (torn)
- 1 sprig fresh rosemary
- 1 tablespoon fresh thyme
- ½ cup fresh basil (chopped)
- 1 teaspoon sea salt
- 1 teaspoon ground black peppercorns
- 3 tablespoons olive oil (divided)

Directions:

Preheat oven to 375°F.

Prepare a 12-inch skillet and heat two tablespoons of the olive oil over medium high heat.

Add in the garlic and sauté for one minute. Add the tomatoes and sauté for 2 minutes before adding the spinach.

Cook for about 2 more minutes, or until spinach is lightly wilted. Remove contents with a slotted spoon and set aside.

Add the remaining oil to the skillet. Once the oil is hot, add the steaks and season with salt and ground black peppercorns.

Sear the steaks on each side, until brown, approximately 7 minutes per side.

Add the tomatoes and spinach back into the pan. Season with rosemary, thyme and basil.

Put the skillet in to the oven and bake until steak reaches desired doneness, approximately 6-10 minutes.

Let rest for 10 minutes before serving.

wwwwwwwwwwwwwwwwwwwwwwwwwwwwwwwwwwwwww

Steak and Eggs Benedict

Take your eggs benedict to another level with this mouth-watering recipe with its spicy hollandaise sauce.

Serves: 4

Total Prep Time: 30 to 50 minutes

Ingredients:

- 8 egg yolks
- 1 tablespoon of black pepper
- 1 tablespoon of salt
- 1 16-ounce Strip Steak
- 3 tablespoons of vegetable oil
- 8 eggs
- 1 French Baguette
- 2 tablespoons of butter
- 1 cup of butter (unsalted)
- 4 tablespoons of lemon juice
- ¼ teaspoon of salt
- ¼ teaspoon of white pepper
- Dash of Hot Pepper

Directions:

Place a skillet on the stove and set to medium high.

Add the oil, and heat until sizzling.

While the oil is heating, combine the black pepper and tablespoon of salt. Mix thoroughly.

Rub the salt mixture onto the steak.

Place the steak into the oil and cook until the steak is medium rare.

The best way to do this is to cook the steak for about 3 to 5 minutes on each side.

Make sure you only turn the steak once to get the best flavoring.

Remove the steak from the heat and allow to cool slightly before slicing it into ½" slices.

While the steak is cooling, slice the baguette into ½" slices. Toast each piece of baguette. Set to the side.

Separate the egg yolks from the egg whites. You can keep the egg whites for a different recipe or throw them away.

In a blender, combine the egg yolks and lemon juice.

Add the hot sauce and blend the mixture for about 20 seconds or until it is well blended.

Make sure you use the lowest setting as you do not want to make the eggs frothy.

Add in the cup of butter, and blend for 2 to 3 minutes or until the butter is fully mixed, and you have a thin mixture.

Blend in the white pepper and ¼ teaspoon of salt. Set aside this mixture as it is a Hollandaise sauce.

In a fresh skillet (the best size is a 10"), add the 2 tablespoons of butter, and place the skillet on the stove set to medium heat.

Once the butter is melted, carefully crack the eggs into the pan.

Don't overcrowd the eggs. You may have to do the eggs in batches.

Cook until the eggs are the desired consistency. With this dish, the yolks should be glossy and the whites should be set.

Remove the eggs from the heat.

Place a few slices of steak onto each baguette toast.

Add a fried egg to the top of the steak. There should only be one egg per baguette toast.

Spoon on the Hollandaise sauce, which is the egg yolk and lemon juice mixture that you made in the blender.

Serve warm.

wwwwwwwwwwwwwwwwwwwwwwwwwwwwwwwwwwwwwww

Old World Chicken Parmesan

This classic Italian dish is sure to impress your friends and family.

Serves: 4

Total Prep Time: 40 minutes

Ingredients:

- 4 chicken breasts (skinless, boneless, pounded thin)
- ¼ cup olive oil
- 3 cloves garlic (crushed and minced)
- ¼ cup shallots (sliced)
- 2 teaspoons fresh rosemary (chopped)
- ¼ cup fresh basil (chopped)
- 2 teaspoons fresh thyme (chopped)
- ¼ cup fresh parsley (chopped)
- 1 teaspoon salt
- 1 teaspoon black pepper
- ¼ cup dry red wine
- 2 ½ cups tomato or marinara sauce
- ½ pound dry vermicelli noodles
- 1 cup fresh mozzarella cheese (shredded)
- ½ cup parmesan cheese (freshly grated)

Directions:

Preheat oven to 450°F.

Prepare a 12-inch skillet and heat the olive oil over medium heat.

Add the chicken and cook on both sides until lightly browned, approximately 2 to 3 minutes per side.

Add the garlic and shallots. Season the chicken with the rosemary, basil, thyme, parsley, salt, and black pepper. Add the red wine and let reduce for 2 minutes.

Add tomato or marinara sauce, stirring gently and spooning over the chicken.

Break the vermicelli noodles in half and spread them around in the sauce. Simmer for 3 minutes and remove from heat.

Top the chicken first with the mozzarella cheese and then the parmesan cheese.

Place in the oven and bake for 20 minutes, or until cheese is bubbly and slightly golden.

Let cool slightly before serving.

wwwwwwwwwwwwwwwwwwwwwwwwwwwwwwwwwwwwwww

Beef and Rosemary Dumplings

Beef and vegetables cooked low and slow, complimented with rosemary flavored dumplings. Very tasty.

Serves: 6

Total Prep Time: 1 hour 20 minutes

Ingredients:

- 2 pounds beef stew meat
- ¼ cup flour
- 1 teaspoon paprika
- 1 teaspoon garlic powder

- 1 teaspoon black pepper
- 1 teaspoon thyme
- 2 tablespoons butter
- 2 cloves garlic (crushed and minced)
- 1 cup red onion (chopped)
- ½ cup celery (diced)
- 2 cups beef stock
- 1 cup apple cider
- 1 cup carrots (chopped)
- 1 cup fresh peas
- 1 cup parsnips (chopped)
- ¼ cup flour
- ¼ cup seasoned bread crumbs
- 2 tablespoons vegetable shortening
- 1 tablespoon fresh rosemary (chopped)
- 1 teaspoon fresh dill (chopped)
- ½ teaspoon salt
- ½ teaspoon black pepper
- 1 egg (beaten)

Directions:

In a bowl combine ¼ cup flour, paprika, garlic powder, black pepper and thyme.

Toss the stew meat pieces into the seasoned flour to coat. Set aside.

Prepare a 12-inch skillet and heat the butter over medium heat. Add the garlic, red onion, and celery. Sauté for 2-3 minutes.

Add the beef and cook until browned, approximately 5 minutes.

Add the beef stock and apple cider, scraping the pan. Increase the heat to medium high and bring to a boil.

Reduce heat to medium low and add the carrots, peas, and parsnips. Cover and simmer for approximately 45 minutes.

While stew is cooking, combine ¼ cup flour, bread crumbs, vegetable shortening, rosemary, dill, salt, black pepper, and egg. Mix until dough forms.

Using tablespoon sized mounds, form the dough into rough ball-shaped dumplings.

Place the dumplings in the stew and cook an additional 15 minutes before serving.

wwwwwwwwwwwwwwwwwwwwwwwwwwwwwwwwwwwww

Chicken Pot Pie

Super easy Chicken Pot Pie made from scratch with a creamy vegetable filling.

Serves: 6

Total Prep Time: 1 hour 50 minutes

Ingredients:

- 4 cups of chicken, cooked and shredded (about 5 to 6 chicken breasts)
- 1/3 cup of butter
- 1 tablespoon of oil
- 2 tablespoons of butter
- 1 cup of carrots (diced)
- mushrooms (1 cup, sliced)
- flour (1/3 cup, all purpose)
- chicken broth (1 ½ cups)
- sweet peas (1 cup, frozen)
- hash browns (2 cups, frozen)
- milk (1 ½ cups)
- 1 ½ teaspoons of Creole seasoning
- 1 onion
- fresh parsley (1/3 cup)
- 1 egg white
- 2 premade piecrusts

Directions:

Add 1 tablespoon of oil to a skillet and place on a stove. Set temperature to medium.

Cut the chicken into smaller strips to help with cooking and add it to the skillet. Fry until the chicken is fully cooked, about 10 to 15 minutes.

Remove from heat and cool.

Once cool, place in a blender, and shred the chicken. Set aside.

Preheat the oven to 350°F.

Place a large saucepan onto the stove and set to medium heat.

Add the 1/3 cup of butter and melt.

Once the butter is melted, stir in the flour. Cook for about 1 minute, stirring continuously.

Stir in the chicken broth.

Add in the milk. Continue to cook until the ingredients become thick; usually about 6 to 7 minutes.

Remove from heat and stir in the Creole seasoning. Set aside.

In a separate skillet, melt 2 tablespoons of butter on a medium-high heat.

Wash, peel, and chop the onions. Place in the skillet.

Wash and chop the mushrooms, add to the onions.

Sauté the mushrooms and onions for about 10 minutes, or until they are tender.

Fold in the shredded chicken.

Wash, peel, and chop the carrots into matchsticks. Add to the onion mixture.

Stir in the peas, and frozen hash browns.

Chop the parsley and mix into the skillet.

Cook for about 2 to 4 minutes until the ingredients are heated.

Pour in the sauce and mix well. Remove from heat.

In a clean and lightly greased, 10" skillet, place one of the piecrusts into the bottom of the skillet.

Remember to remove the pie plate if it is sold with one.

Pour the chicken mixture into the piecrust until it is filled.

Top with the remaining piecrust, again, making sure you remove the pie plate if it has one.

Separate the egg white from the egg yolk. Throw away the egg yolk or use it for a different recipe.

Brush the egg white over the top pie crust.

Cut 5 slits into the top of the pie.

Place in the oven for 1 hour or until the pie crust is golden brown and the mixture is bubbling.

Serve warm.

Farm House Breakfast

A classic, healthy and hearty breakfast to start your day.

Serves: 4

Total Prep Time: 50 minutes

Ingredients:

- 3 cups of red skinned potatoes
- 8 eggs
- ¼ cup of parsley leaves (chopped and fresh)
- ¼ teaspoon of black pepper
- 3 tablespoons of butter
- 1 teaspoon of salt
- 2 garlic cloves
- 1 cup of farmhouse cheddar (shredded)

Directions:

Preheat the oven to 400°F.

Wash the potatoes, but do not peel them.

Chop the potatoes into small hash browns, usually smaller than a half inch.

Wash and chop the parsley leaves.

Place a 10" to 12" skillet onto the stove and set the heat to medium.

Add the butter and allow the butter to melt completely.

Place the potatoes into the butter, and sauté for about 15 minutes or until the potatoes are tender and have started to brown.

Mince the garlic, and stir into the potatoes, cook for an additional minute.

Fold in the salt and pepper.

Add the parsley, cook for another minute.

Remove the Skillet pan from the stove.

Using the back of a wooden spoon, create an indent into the potato. Make 4 indents; one for two eggs.

Carefully break two eggs into each indentation.

Place in the oven, and bake until the egg whites are cooked, roughly 10 minutes.

Once the eggs have the consistency you want, shred the farmhouse cheese.

Remove the skillet from the oven and sprinkle the cheese over the eggs.

Return to the oven and bake for 1 to 2 minutes or until the cheese has melted.

Remove from the oven and serve warm.

wwwwwwwwwwwwwwwwwwwwwwwwwwwwwwwwwwwwwwww

Crispy Coconut Chicken Tenders

An easy weeknight meal and a fantastic appetizer!

Serve: 4

Total Prep Time: 25 minutes

Ingredients:

- 4 x 4-ounce chicken breast (skinless, boneless)
- 1½ cups flour
- ½ cup shredded coconut
- 2 tablespoons milk
- 2 eggs
- 1 teaspoon oregano
- 1 teaspoon paprika
- 1 teaspoon thyme
- 1 teaspoon salt and black pepper
- Extra virgin olive oil

Directions:

Whisk eggs in a bowl, add milk and mix.

In another shallow bowl, combine flour with spices.

In a third shallow bowl, place the shredded coconut.

Slice chicken breast into 2"-wide chicken strips.

Dip each strip in egg mixture, then coat with flour mixture, next drip in coconut mixture.

In a deep skillet, heat 4 tablespoons oil over medium heat. Drop chicken strips into skillet and cook for 3-4 minutes per side or when they are no longer pink inside.

Serve with lemon garlic dipping sauce below.

wwwwwwwwwwwwwwwwwwwwwwwwwwwwwwwwwwwwwwww

Lemon Garlic Dipping Sauce

This sauce is super delicious, tangy, creamy and just right.

Serve: 6

Total Prep Time: 7 minutes

Ingredients:

- 1 cup mayonnaise
- 1/3 cup lemon juice
- 2 cloves garlic, grated
- 1 teaspoon black pepper (coarse)
- 1 teaspoon salt

Directions:

Place ingredients in blender and mix until smooth.

Refrigerate for 30 minutes before serving.

wwwwwwwwwwwwwwwwwwwwwwwwwwwwwwwwwwwwwwww

Spicy Potato Hash Browns

A quick, healthy and nutritious side dish.

Serves: 4

Total Prep Time: 1 hour

Ingredients:

- 5 baking potatoes
- ¼ teaspoon of black pepper
- ¼ teaspoon of onion powder
- ½ teaspoon of salt
- ¼ teaspoon of thyme (dried)
- 1 teaspoon of fresh thyme
- ¼ cup of vegetable oil
- ¼ teaspoon of oregano
- ½ teaspoon of garlic powder
- 2 teaspoons of minced garlic
- 1 cup of yellow onion (diced)
- 3 tablespoons of butter
- ¼ teaspoon of cayenne pepper

Directions:

Wash the potatoes and place them in a pot.

Fill with water and place on the stove which is set to high.

Bring to a boil; cook the potatoes until they are half cooked, roughly about 15 minutes after the water boils.

Drain the water and allow the potatoes to cool.

Remove the skins from the potatoes while they are still warm.

Chop the potatoes into ½" hash browns.

Wash, peel and dice the yellow onions.

Mince the fresh garlic

Place the 12" skillet onto the stove and set the temperature to high.

Pour in the oil.

Add the butter and heat thoroughly. Add the onions.

Sauté the onions until tender, roughly about 3 to 5 minutes.

Add the minced garlic to the onions, stirring for about a minute or until the smell of garlic grows strong.

Fold in the potatoes and stir until the potatoes are mixed well with the onions.

Chop the fresh thyme and add it to the potatoes along with the salt and pepper.

Sprinkle on the dried thyme, oregano, onion powder, garlic powder and cayenne pepper. Do not stir in the ingredients. Simply shake the pan to keep the potatoes from burning.

Allow the ingredients to cook until the bottom of the potatoes is golden brown, roughly about 4 to 6 minutes.

Using a spatula, turn the potatoes.

Cook on the other side until the potatoes are golden brown throughout, roughly an additional 4 minutes.

Remove from heat and serve warm.

wwwwwwwwwwwwwwwwwwwwwwwwwwwwwwwwwwwwwwww

Skillet One-Pot Chicken

The easiest one-pot chicken meal ever with a rich flavor too.

Serves: 4

Total Prep Time: 35 minutes

Ingredients:

- 1 ½ pounds chicken breast (boneless, skinless)
- 1 tablespoon olive oil
- 1 cup red onion (sliced)
- 2 cups small red potatoes (halved)
- 2 cups sugar snap peas (washed and trimmed)
- 3 cloves garlic (crushed and minced)
- 1 cup chicken stock
- ¼ cup balsamic vinegar
- ¼ cup heavy cream
- 1 tablespoon honey
- 1 sprig fresh rosemary
- ¼ cup fresh basil (chopped)
- 1 teaspoon salt
- 1 teaspoon black pepper

Directions:

Preheat oven to 400°F.

Prepare a 12-inch skillet and heat the olive oil over medium heat.

Add the chicken and brown on both sides, approximately 3-5 minutes per side. Remove from pan and set aside.

Add the red potatoes, sugar snap peas, and garlic. Sauté just until potatoes begin to brown, approximately 5 minutes. Add more olive oil, if needed. Remove from the pan and keep with the chicken.

Add the balsamic vinegar to the pan and reduce, scraping the skillet while you do so, for 1-2 minutes.

Stir in the chicken stock, heavy cream and honey, stirring constantly. Season with rosemary, basil, salt, and black pepper.

Add the chicken back to the skillet, followed by the vegetables.

Place the skillet in the oven and bake 20 minutes or until chicken is cooked through and juices run clear.

wwwwwwwwwwwwwwwwwwwwwwwwwwwwwwwwwww

Beef and Potato Pie

This is a popular variety of pie eaten in England. A comforting homemade pie. Perfect for the entire family.

Serves: 6

Total Prep Time: 1 hour 35 minutes

Ingredients:

- 1 ½ pounds of ground beef
- 1 tablespoon of canola oil
- ¾ cup of beef broth
- 3 tablespoons of flour
- ½ teaspoon of salt
- 1 onion
- 3 red potatoes
- 1 egg
- 1 premade pie shell

Directions:

Preheat the oven to 375°F.

Place a 10" skillet onto the stove. Set the temperature to medium high.

Add the oil and heat.

Wash, peel and chop the onions. Add to the oil, and cook until the onions are tender, about 3 to 5 minutes.

Fold in the ground beef and cook until the meat is browned, about 10 to 15 minutes.

While the ground beef is cooking, wash and chop the potatoes into ½" cubes.

Fold the potatoes into the cooked beef and cook for an additional minute.

Remove from the stove and drain the grease from the meat.

Set the stove to medium-low and return the skillet to the stove.

Sprinkle the beef with flour and stir until it is fully blended.

Add the beef broth and mix.

Simmer for 2 to 3 minutes or until the sauce begins to thicken.

Stir in the salt and remove from heat.

Remove the pie shell from its aluminum plate.

Place the dough on top of the beef mixture.

Whisk the egg in a separate bowl and brush the mixture over the pie crust.

Cut 2 to 3 slits into the middle of the dough.

Place the skillet into the oven and bake until the crust is golden-brown, and the mixture is bubbling, about 45 minutes.

Remove from oven and let stand for 10 minutes.

Serve warm.

wwwwwwwwwwwwwwwwwwwwwwwwwwwwwwwwwwwwwwwwwww

Honey Garlic Chicken Thighs with Broccoli Slaw

A favorite dinner choice for many. Very easy to make and loaded with flavor.

Serves: 4

Total Prep Time: 45 minutes

Ingredients:

- 8 chicken thighs (skinless, boneless)
- ½ cup honey
- 6 cloves garlic (minced)
- 1 cup low-sodium chicken stock
- ¼ cup soy sauce
- Extra virgin olive oil
- Broccoli Slaw:
- 1 head broccoli
- ½ cup carrots (grated)
- ¼ cup raisins
- ¼ cup peanuts or cashews
- ½ cup low-fat mayonnaise
- 1 teaspoon black pepper
- ½ teaspoon salt

Directions:

Heat 3 tablespoons olive oil in a large skillet over medium heat. Add chicken thighs, and brown.

Add garlic, honey, and soy sauce, stir to coat thighs. Cook thighs about a minute per side in honey sauce.

Add chicken stock, bring to simmer, reduce heat to medium-low, cover with a lid or foil and cook for 25 minutes or until chicken is no longer pink inside.

For slaw, peel broccoli stalk and grate broccoli using food processor.

Combine grated broccoli with remaining ingredients and refrigerate for 20 minutes before serving.

Serve Honey Garlic Chicken Thighs with Broccoli Slaw.

WWWWWWWWWWWWWWWWWWWWWWWWWWWWWWWWWWWWW

Breakfast Scramble

A healthy and nutritious protein dish, colorful and well flavored. A suitable breakfast choice.

Serves: 6

Total Prep Time: 15 minutes

Ingredients:

- 12 eggs
- 1 red onion
- 1 jalapeno
- 2 tablespoons of chives (diced)
- 2 tablespoons of butter (unsalted)
- ¼ teaspoon of salt
- ¼ teaspoon of black pepper
- ½ cup of goat cheese (½ cup of feta cheese or cheddar cheese as a substitute for goat cheese)

Directions:

Place a large 12" skillet on the stove and set the heat to medium.

Wash, peel, and dice the red onion.

Wash and cut the jalapeno into circles. Keep the seeds with the cut pepper.

Add the butter to the skillet and melt.

Pour in the onion and jalapeno and sauté for about 5 to 7 minutes or until the peppers and onions are soft.

In a separate bowl, whisk together the eggs.

Whisk in the salt and pepper.

Pour the eggs into the skillet and cook, stirring frequently, until you have the desired consistency, roughly 3 to 5 minutes.

While the eggs are cooking, crumble the goat cheese. If you are using cheddar cheese, shred it, or crumble the feta cheese.

Wash and dice the fresh chives.

Remove the eggs from the stove and fold in the cheese and chives.

Serve warm.

wwwwwwwwwwwwwwwwwwwwwwwwwwwwwwwwwwwww

Berry Pancakes

Try this delicious pancake served with crispy bacon. Loved by many, especially children.

Serves: 4

Total Prep Time: 30 minutes

Ingredients:

- 1 cup of flour (all-purpose}
- ¼ cup of white sugar
- 1 cup of milk
- 2 tablespoons of butter (unsalted)
- 4 eggs
- ¼ teaspoon of salt
- ½ teaspoon of lemon zest
- ½ cup of blueberries
- ½ cup of raspberries

Directions:

Preheat the oven to 400°F.

Sift the flour into a bowl.

Zest the lemon, then add it to the flour.

Add the salt.

In a separate bowl, whisk together the eggs and milk.

Slowly add the egg mixture to the flour mixture. Mix until the ingredients are well blended and you have a smooth batter.

Wash and stem the blueberries. Place in a separate bowl.

Wash and cut the raspberries in half. Place the raspberries in the same bowl as the blueberries and toss the fruit together.

Place a skillet onto the stove and set the heat to high. Make sure that you use a 12" skillet.

When the skillet is hot, add the butter and allow it to melt.

Once the butter is melted, pour the batter into the hot skillet. Turn the skillet slightly to make sure the batter covers the entire pan.

Add the berry mixture to the top of the batter. You should scatter the berries so they are all over the entire batter. Don't worry if the berries sink into the batter.

Remove from the stove and place the skillet into the oven.

Bake for 20 minutes or until the pastry is baked completely through and is puffed.

Remove from the oven, serve warm with syrup, icing sugar or whipped cream.

WWWWWWWWWWWWWWWWWWWWWWWWWWWWWWWWWWW

Chicken and Dressings

Chicken and Dressings bring the flavor of Thanksgiving to a weeknight dinner.

Serves: 6

Total Prep Time: 1 hour 5 minutes

Ingredients:

- 3 cups of chicken (cubed)
- 1 teaspoon of salt
- 1 teaspoon of pepper
- 1 cup of celery
- 2 eggs
- 1 cup of frozen corn
- 1 cup of onion (chopped)
- 2 tablespoons of butter
- 1 /12 teaspoon of poultry seasoning
- 2 packages of Buttermilk Cornbread Mix (6ounce packages)
- 2 tablespoons of vegetable oil
- 1 ¾ cups of milk

Directions:

Preheat the oven to 400°F.

Wash, peel and chop onion.

Wash and chop celery.

In a bowl, toss together the salt, pepper and raw chicken.

Add 1 tablespoon of oil to a skillet and place on a stove. Set temperature to medium.

Cube the chicken and add it to the skillet. Fry until the chicken is fully cooked, about 10 to 15 minutes.

Remove chicken from heat and set aside to cool.

Add the butter to a 10" skillet. You can use the one you cooked the chicken in or a clean skillet.

Melt the butter on medium heat.

Toss the onion and celery together then add to the skillet.

Cook for about 10 minutes or until the celery and onions are tender.

Remove from heat and pour the celery mixture into a bowl. Set aside.

Pour the oil into the skillet and place in the oven.

Heat for 5 minutes.

While the skillet is heating, mix together the cornbread and chicken.

Fold in the poultry seasoning.

Toss in the onions and celery.

Add the corn and toss until all the ingredients are well blended.

In a separate bowl, whisk together the milk and eggs.

Add it to the vegetable mixture and mix well.

Remove the skillet from the oven.

Pour the vegetable batter into the skillet.

Place back in the oven and bake for 30 to 35 minutes. You will want the dish to be golden brown.

Serve warm.

WWWWWWWWWWWWWWWWWWWWWWWWWWWWWWWWWWWWWW

Roasted Rosemary Chicken

This is a simple way to roast chicken, but it gives you that sweet roast flavor and the rosemary gives it a sweet taste blended with the garlic and butter.

Serves: 6

Total Prep Time: 1 hour 40 minutes

Ingredients:

- 1 large roasting chicken (4-5 pounds)
- 6 fresh rosemary sprigs
- 1 teaspoon of paprika
- 1 tablespoons of kosher salt
- ¼ cup of olive oil
- 1 teaspoon dry thyme
- 2 tablespoons of lemon juice
- 2 tablespoons of butter
- ¼ teaspoon of sea salt
- 2 teaspoons of minced garlic
- 24 pearl onions (trimmed)
- 1 cup dry white wine
- 12 white mushrooms (trimmed and quartered)

Directions:

Pre-heat the oven to 450°F

Rinse your chicken inside out with cold running water. Use paper towels to pat dry the chicken inside and out. Chicken must be dry if you want a crispy skinned chicken.

Season the cavity of the chicken with the kosher salt and place two of the rosemary sprigs inside.

Chop rosemary of two sprigs.

Mix the chopped rosemary, garlic, olive oil, pepper, paprika, lemon juice and thyme in a small mixing bowl. Stir until well combined.

Place your largest skillet on the stove and set to medium high.

Add the butter. Add the pearl onions when the butter is melted. Sauté the onions until they are fragrant and almost tender, about 3-4 minutes. Remove from heat.

Place the chicken, breasts side up, in the skillet, pushing the onions on the side.

Add the mushrooms. Brush generously the chicken and mushrooms with the rosemary and olive oil mixture. Place two rosemary sprigs on the chicken. Tie the chicken legs with kitchen twine.

Place the skillet in the pre-heated oven. Let the chicken roast for 1h15, until the chicken is well cooked and the juices run clear when you slit the thigh skin.

To make certain your chicken is well cook, insert a meat thermometer in the breast without touching any bones. The internal temperature should read 165°F.

Remove the chicken from the oven and place the chicken on a serving plate with the onions and mushrooms while you prepare the sauce.

Cover the chicken loosely with aluminum foil to keep it warm.

Place the skillet on the stove on high heat and quickly add the white wine.

Bring to a boil. Let the sauce reduce by half. It should take about 5 minutes.

Make sure to scrap all the bits of flavor from the chicken and the onions from the bottom of the skillet with a spoon as the sauce is reducing. Keep the sauce warm until ready to serve.

When ready to serve, carve your chicken and place the sauce in a saucer. Serve warm with pearl onions and mushrooms.

wwwwwwwwwwwwwwwwwwwwwwwwwwwwwwwwwwwwwwww

Spicy Chicken and Lemongrass Peanut Noodles

This is a healthy comfort food dish and a crowd favorite.

Serves: 4

Total Prep Time: 30 minutes

Ingredients:

- 1-pound boneless skinless chicken breast (cubed)
- 2 teaspoons olive oil
- ½ cup soy sauce
- 3 cloves garlic (crushed and minced)
- 1 tablespoon fresh ginger (grated)
- 1 tablespoon fresh lemongrass (chopped)
- 1 tablespoon chili garlic paste
- ½ cup creamy natural peanut butter
- 1 tablespoon lime juice
- 2 teaspoons sesame oil
- 2 cups chicken stock
- ½ pound angel hair pasta
- ½ cup peanuts (chopped)
- Scallions (sliced for garnish)

Directions:

Prepare a 12-inch skillet and add the olive oil over medium heat.

Add the chicken and sauté until browned, approximately 5 minutes.

Add the soy sauce, garlic, ginger, lemon grass, and chili garlic paste. Stir in with the chicken and cook 1-2 minutes.

Add the peanut butter, lime juice, sesame oil, and chicken stock. Turn heat up to medium high until the stock boils. Add the angel hair pasta and reduce the heat to simmer. Cook 5-7 minutes, or until noodles are tender.

Remove from heat and add peanuts before serving.

wwwwwwwwwwwwwwwwwwwwwwwwwwwwwwwwwwwww

Kung Pao Chicken

Put some spice in this restaurant favorite by preparing it from scratch. This highly addictive dish continues to be one of the most popular Chinese dish in America.

Serves: 4

Total Prep Time: 30 minutes

Ingredients

- 4 x 4-ounce chicken breast (skinless, boneless)
- 1 teaspoon fresh ginger (grated)
- ½ cup shallots (diced)
- ½ cup low-sodium soy sauce
- 2 teaspoons brown sugar
- ½ teaspoon cornstarch
- 1 green chili pepper (seeded, minced)
- Extra virgin olive oil

Directions:

Cube chicken into ¾" pieces.

Heat 4 tablespoons oil in a deep skillet over medium heat, add chicken breast and brown. Remove from skillet and set aside.

Into same skillet, add shallots, ginger, pepper; sauté for 2 minutes, ensure ginger does not brown too quickly.

Stir in cornstarch and brown sugar, pour in a little soy sauce to deglaze skillet. Return chicken to skillet, mix in corn starch.

Reduce heat and simmer on low for 10 minutes.

Serve Kung Pao Chicken with white rice.

wwwwwwwwwwwwwwwwwwwwwwwwwwwwwwwwwwwwwww

Skillet Lasagna

This ultimate, comforting and cheesy meal is very classic. Great meal for when friends are visiting.

Serves: 6

Total Prep Time: 1 hour

Ingredients:

- 1-pound ground beef
- 1 tablespoon dried basil
- 1 red onion
- 1 white onion
- 1 tablespoon shallot flakes
- 2 tablespoons dried oregano
- 1 box ready to use lasagna noodles
- 3 garlic cloves
- 8 cups pasta sauce
- ½ cup Parmesan cheese
- 2 cups mozzarella cheese (shredded)

Directions:

Preheat the oven to 375°F.

Place the ground beef into your skillet.

Brown the beef over medium-high temperatures until it is cooked.

Wash, peel and chop the red and white onions.

Add in the onions to the beef and then cook until they are fragrant and tender.

Drain the beef to remove excess grease.

In a separate bowl, whisk together the pasta sauce and parmesan cheese.

Add the shallot flakes.

Mince the garlic and add to the pasta sauce, mix well.

Pour the pasta sauce over the meat.

Reduce heat to low and simmer as you prepare your lasagna.

Coat a large, 12 to 15-inch skillet with non-stick spray. You can also use a smaller 8-inch skillet to make personal sized lasagna.

Pour two cups of the meat sauce into the bottom of the skillet. Spread it out so there is an even layer of sauce.

Separate the box of noodles into 3 equal parts and then place 1/3 of the noodles onto the sauce in the skillet. Break the noodles as needed.

When the sauce is covered with noodles, spoon on another 2 cups of meat sauce.

Shred the mozzarella cheese.

Sprinkle 1/3 of cheese over the sauce.

Take the second third of noodles and cover the mozzarella. Repeat until you've used all of the noodles.

Pour the remaining sauce onto the last layer of noodles.

Cover with the remaining cheese.

Use aluminum foil to cover the lasagna and bake for roughly 20 to 25 minutes.

Remove the foil and then cook for 10 more minutes or until the cheese is golden.

Remove from the oven and allow to slightly cool before serving warm.

wwwwwwwwwwwwwwwwwwwwwwwwwwwwwwwwwwww

Skillet Cheeseburgers

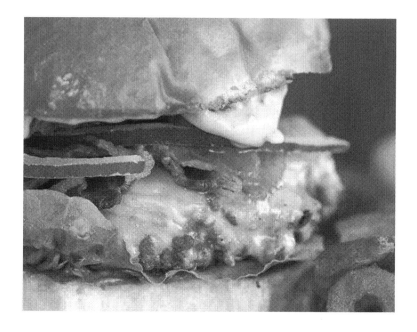

These Skillet Cheeseburgers are flavorful, tender and moist.
Perfect for the children's lunch box and your picnic baskets.

Serves: 4

Total Prep Time: 30 to 50 minutes

Ingredients:

- 1 ½ pounds of ground beef
- 1 ½ teaspoons of canola oil
- 1 teaspoon of black pepper
- 2 teaspoons of garlic salt
- ¼ teaspoon of paprika
- ½ cup of onions
- 1 egg
- ¼ cup of bread crumbs
- 4 slices of cheddar cheese
- 4 hamburger buns

Directions:

Wash, peel and dice the onions.

Place the paprika, garlic salt, and black pepper.

Whisk together until well blended.

Add the onions.

Place in the ground beef.

Carefully crack the egg into the ground beef.

Add the breadcrumbs.

Mix the ingredients by hand until the ingredients are fully mixed and the meat clings together.

Form the meat into 4 burgers.

Pour the oil into a 12" skillet.

Place on the stove and set the temperature to medium-high.

Grill the burgers for 3 to 5 minutes on each side, flipping only once, until they are cooked the way you want.

Slice the cheese while the burgers are cooking.

Place one or two slices of cheese on each burger when they are fully cooked.

Remove from heat.

Serve on a bun with your favorite toppings.

wwwwwwwwwwwwwwwwwwwwwwwwwwwwwwwwwwwwwww

Mexican Skillet Casserole

Bring the Mexican flavors to your family dinner table with this delicious Mexican Skillet Casserole.

Serves: 6

Total Prep Time: 30 to 40 minutes

Ingredients:

- 1 pound of ground beef
- 2 teaspoons of canola oil
- ¾ cup of salt
- 2 tablespoons of chili powder
- 4 garlic cloves
- 2 cups of black beans (1 -15ounce can)
- 1 teaspoon of cumin (ground)
- 1 ¾ cups of onion (chopped)
- 2 cups of diced tomatoes with jalapenos (1- 15ounce can)
- ½ cup of cheddar cheese (shredded)
- 1 ¾ cups of white rice (cooked)

Directions:

Cook the rice according to the instructions on the package.

In a 10" skillet, add the oil.

Place on the stove, set to medium-high heat, and heat the oil.

Wash, peel, and chop the onion, add it to the skillet.

Mince the garlic and add to the onion. Stir until it is well blended.

Sauté the vegetables until the onions are tender, about 3 to 5 minutes.

When the onions are tender, add the ground beef. Cook until it is brown, about 10 to 15 minutes.

Drain the beef, return the beef to the skillet and the stove.

Fold in the cumin.

Add the salt and chili powder.

Stir until the ingredients are thoroughly incorporated.

Drain the tomatoes, and add to the beef, mix well.

Drain and rinse the black beans and stir until they are dispersed through the meat.

Fold in the rice, making sure the ingredients are well blended.

Cook for an additional 2 to 5 minutes or until the dish is heated.

Shred the cheese and add to the top of the meat.

Cover with a lid and allow to cook for another 2 minutes.

Remove from heat and serve warm.

wwwwwwwwwwwwwwwwwwwwwwwwwwwwwwwwwwwww

Beef Stroganoff

This retro classic Beef Stroganoff is simple, juicy and smothered in a creamy sauce. A great weeknight meal.

Serves: 6

Total Prep Time: 1 hour 30 minutes

Ingredients:

- 2 pounds of beef roast (chuck)
- 1 onion
- 3 garlic cloves
- ½ cup of red wine
- 1 1/3 cups of beef broth
- ¼ cup of flour (all-purpose)
- 4 tablespoons of butter
- ¼ cup of butter
- 1 teaspoon of salt
- ½ teaspoon of black pepper
- 1 tablespoon of Worcestershire sauce
- sour cream (1/3 cup)
- olive oil (1 tablespoon)
- 1 teaspoon of yellow mustard
- mushrooms (1 cup, sliced)
- cream cheese (1/3 cup)
- red pepper flakes (2 teaspoons, crushed)

Directions:

Slice the chuck roast into 1 ½" strips.

Place the strips into a bowl.

Pour the red wine over it.

Add the salt and black pepper. Toss until the beef is coated. Place in the refrigerator and let it marinate for about 10 minutes. Don't overly marinate this dish.

After 10 minutes, remove the chuck beef and pat dry. Do not throw away the marinade.

Place a skillet (a 12" skillet works best) onto the stove and set the temperature to medium.

Heat the olive oil in the skillet.

Once the oil is hot, add the beef strips. Fry until the strips are brown, stirring occasionally. This usually takes about 5 to 7 minutes.

Remove the beef and set aside.

Drain the grease out of the skillet and return it to the stove.

Add 2 tablespoons of butter to the skillet and melt.

Wash, peel, and chop the onion.

Mince the garlic, and add the onion and garlic to the skillet.

Cook until the onion is tender, about 3 to 5 minutes.

Once the onions are cooked, remove them, and place them in the same dish as the beef.

Return the skillet to the stove.

Add in 2 tablespoons of butter and heat it until it melts.

Wash and slice the mushrooms.

Stir the mushrooms into the butter. Cook them until they are tender, stirring frequently, usually 7 to 10 minutes.

Remove the mushrooms from the heat, and place in a separate bowl. Do not add it to the beef.

Return the skillet to the stove.

Add the ¼ cup of butter, and heat until it melts.

When the butter has melted, whisk in the flour. Cook for 4 minutes, stirring constantly.

Stir in the beef stock and bring the butter mixture to a boil.

When it is boiling, reduce the heat to medium-low. Make sure that you are constantly stirring during this time or your sauce will burn.

Pour in the Worcestershire sauce.

Add the mustard.

Stir in the marinade that you had saved.

Fold in the red pepper flakes.

Stir until the ingredients are completely incorporated.

Add the beef and onion mixture.

Cover the skillet with a lid and simmer for 50 to 60 minutes. Cook until the meat is tender, stirring occasionally.

When the beef is tender, whisk together the sour cream and cream cheese until smooth.

Fold in the mushrooms.

Add the mushroom mixture to the beef mixture and cook for an additional 5 minutes.

Serve warm.

wwwwwwwwwwwwwwwwwwwwwwwwwwwwwwwwwwwwwwwwwww

Dijon and Wine Roasted Chicken

This Dijon and Wine Roasted Chicken is the best roasted chicken ever. Try it!

Serves: 4-6

Total Prep Time: 1 hour 15 minutes

Ingredients:

- 2 pounds assorted chicken pieces (bone-in, with skin)
- ½ cup pancetta (cubed)
- ¼ cup shallots (sliced)
- 2 cup Brussels sprouts (halved)
- ¼ cup Dijon mustard
- 1 tablespoon Herbs de Provence
- 1 teaspoon salt
- 1 teaspoon ground peppercorns
- ½ cup flour
- 1 cup chicken stock
- ½ cup dry white wine

Directions:

Preheat the oven to 350°F.

Prepare a 12-inch skillet and add the pancetta over medium heat. Cook the pancetta until crispy, approximately 5 minutes.

Add the shallots and cook while stirring for 1-2 minutes more before adding the Brussels sprouts and cooking, stirring frequently, for an additional five minutes.

Using a slotted spoon, remove the Brussels sprouts, shallots and pancetta. Set aside.

In a bowl, combine the Herbs de Provence, salt and ground peppercorns with the flour. Mix well.

Brush the chicken with the Dijon mustard and then dredge lightly in the flour mixture.

Place the chicken back in the skillet and using the residual grease from the pancetta (add additional olive oil, if needed) brown the chicken on both sides over medium heat.

Add the white wine and reduce for 2 minutes, then add the chicken stock to the skillet followed by the Brussels sprouts and pancetta.

Place the skillet in the oven and bake for 35-40 minutes, or until chicken is crispy brown and cooked through to at least 165°F internal temperature.

Transfer to serving plates and drizzle with pan sauce before serving.

wwwwwwwwwwwwwwwwwwwwwwwwwwwwwwwwwwwwwww

Sunny Skillet Breakfast

This hearty breakfast recipe can easily be changed to suit your preference with the addition of some of your favorite vegetables or meats.

Serves: 6

Total Prep Time: 40 minutes

Ingredients:

- 3 cups of potatoes
- 2 tablespoons of vegetable oil
- 1 onion
- 1 red bell pepper
- 6 eggs
- 1 garlic clove
- 1 tablespoon of butter
- ¼ teaspoon of pepper

Directions:

Preheat the oven to 350°F.

Wash and peel the potatoes.

Shred the potatoes and place in a bowl of cold water so the potatoes are completely covered. Let them sit for 5 minutes.

While the potatoes are sitting, place a skillet onto the stove. The best size to use for this meal is a 10" pan.

Add the butter and set the heat to medium.

Pour in the oil. Heat the oil and butter.

Wash and seed the bell pepper. Dice it into small portions.

Wash, peel, and chop the onion.

Place both vegetables into the hot pan, and sauté until the onions are tender, roughly 3 to 5 minutes.

When the onions are cooked, mince the garlic, and add to the onion mixture. Sauté for a minute.

Remove the potatoes from the water and drain them on a paper towel. Place the shredded potatoes into the pan and mix until the onion mixture is well blended.

Continue to grill until the potatoes are golden brown and tender, roughly about 10 minutes.

Once the potatoes are tender, remove from the heat.

Using the back of a wooden spoon, create an indentation in the potato. Make 6 indents; one for each egg.

Carefully break an egg into each indentation.

Sprinkle the eggs with pepper.

Place the skillet into the oven and bake the dish for 12 to 14 minutes or until the eggs are the desired consistency.

Remove from the oven and serve warm.

wwwwwwwwwwwwwwwwwwwwwwwwwwwwwwwwwwwwwww

Greek Beef Stew

This Greek Beef Stew is packed with carrots, potatoes, tomatoes and seasonings and some red wine for added flavor.

Serves: 5-6

Total Prep Time: 1 hour 10 minutes

Ingredients:

- 2 pounds beef chuck (boneless)
- 4 small white potatoes (cubed)
- 1 cup carrots (sliced)
- 1 onion (sliced)
- 4 cups low-sodium beef stock
- ½ cup red wine
- 2 tablespoons flour
- 1 teaspoon oregano
- Salt, black pepper
- Extra virgin olive oil

Directions:

Slice beef chuck into 1½" cubes, massage meat with 2 teaspoons salt and 2 teaspoons black pepper.

Heat 3 tablespoons extra virgin olive oil in large skillet pot over medium heat, add beef and brown.

Remove beef from pot onto plate.

Add onions, bell pepper, and sauté until onions are translucent.

Mix in flour and stir in wine.

Add beef stock, oregano, return beef to pot.

Lower heat to low.

Add potato, carrots, cover and simmer for an hour.

wwwwwwwwwwwwwwwwwwwwwwwwwwwwwwwwwwwwwwww

Caprese Skillet Eggs

Very colorful, tasty and nourishing. A great breakfast choice.

Serves: 4

Total Prep Time: 30 minutes

Ingredients:

- 3 tomatoes
- ½ cup of onion (chopped)
- 4 eggs
- 2 tablespoons of olive oil
- ½ teaspoon of salt
- 4 teaspoons of fresh oregano
- 4 teaspoons of fresh chives
- 4 teaspoons of fresh basil
- ½ teaspoon of pepper
- ½ cup of mozzarella cheese

Directions:

Wash the tomatoes, and chop into bite-sized pieces.

Wash, peel and chop the onion.

Place a 10" skillet onto the stove and set to medium heat.

Pour in the oil and heat.

Once the oil is hot, place in the chopped onion.

Sauté the onion until it is tender and almost translucent; between 3 to 5 minutes.

Fold in the tomatoes and season with the salt and pepper.

Cook the vegetables for about 5 minutes, or until the tomatoes are soft. Stir frequently while cooking.

Once the tomatoes are soft, use a wooden spoon to make an indentation in the tomato mixture.

Repeat until you have four wells or indentations in the tomatoes.

Carefully crack an egg into each well.

Place a lid on the skillet and continue cooking until the whites are firm and the yolks are still soft. This can take anywhere from 5 to 10 minutes.

Shred the mozzarella cheese

Once the eggs are the desired consistency, sprinkle the dish with the shredded cheese.

Return the lid to the skillet and cook for an additional minute.

Wash and chop the oregano, basil, and chives. Toss together.

Remove from heat and sprinkle the herbs on top.

Serve on its own or with toast.

wwwwwwwwwwwwwwwwwwwwwwwwwwwwwwwwwwww

Spinach Stuffed Sundried Tomato Chicken

Try this juicy stuffed chicken breast with the sweet flavor of sun-dried tomato and cheese, yummy!

Serves: 4

Total Prep Time: 55 minutes

Ingredients:

- 4 chicken breasts (boneless, skinless, split along the side)
- ½ cup bacon (diced)
- 2 cloves garlic (crushed and minced)
- 2 cups spinach (chopped)
- ½ cup jarred sundried tomatoes (chopped)
- 1 cup seasoned bread crumbs
- ½ cup parmesan cheese (freshly grated)
- ¼ cup fresh parsley (chopped)
- 2 eggs (beaten)
- 1 teaspoon salt
- 1 teaspoon black pepper
- 1 cup red onion (chopped)
- 4 cups sweet potato (cubed)
- ¼ teaspoon nutmeg
- ¼ teaspoon oregano
- ½ teaspoon paprika
- 1 tablespoon olive oil
- 1 cup chicken stock
- 1 cup smoked provolone cheese (shredded)

wwwwwwwwwwwwwwwwwwwwwwwwwwwwwwwwwwwww

Directions:

Preheat oven to 375°F.

Prepare a 12-inch skillet and add the bacon over medium heat. Cook until bacon is semi crisp, approximately 5 minutes.

Add the garlic and then sauté for one minute before adding the spinach and sundried tomatoes.

Sauté, stirring gently for 2-3 minutes. Use a slotted spoon to transfer the mixture to a bowl and set aside to cool slightly.

Add the sweet potatoes and onion to the skillet and cook, stirring occasionally, for 5 minutes.

Season with nutmeg, oregano, and paprika. Cook an additional 3 minutes before removing from the pan. Add the olive oil to the pan and keep the heat on medium.

In a bowl, combine the seasoned bread crumbs, parmesan cheese, fresh parsley, salt and black pepper.

Stuff each chicken breast with the equal amounts of the spinach mixture.

Baste each piece of chicken with the beaten egg and then dredge through the bread crumb mixture.

Place the chicken in the pan and cook until lightly browned on each side, approximately 3-4 minutes.

Add the sweet potatoes back into the pan and add the chicken stock. Cover the chicken with shredded provolone cheese.

Place the skillet in the oven and then bake for 20-25 minutes, or until chicken is cooked through and juices run clear. Enjoy!

wwwwwwwwwwwwwwwwwwwwwwwwwwwwwwwwwwwwww

Conclusion

Congrats on completing all 30 delicious Skillet Recipes! We hope you enjoyed all 30 recipes and that they were easy to whip up and tasty.

So, what happens next?

In order to become better at making skillets you will have to practice. Be sure to keep cooking and enjoying all the delicious recipes featured in this Creative Skillet Cookbook. All of which will be easy to follow and can be created in a hassle-free environment. So, whenever you feel like you have mastered all the recipes in this book, grab another one of our books and let your culinary creativity run wild.

Remember, drop us a review if you loved what you read and until we meet again, keep on cooking delicious food.

WWWWWWWWWWWWWWWWWWWWWWWWWWWWWWWWW

About the Author

Born in New Germantown, Pennsylvania, Stephanie Sharp received a Masters degree from Penn State in English Literature. Driven by her passion to create culinary masterpieces, she applied and was accepted to The International Culinary School of the Art Institute where she excelled in French cuisine. She has married her cooking skills with an aptitude for business by opening her own small cooking school where she teaches students of all ages.

Stephanie's talents extend to being an author as well and she has written over 400 e-books on the art of cooking and baking that include her most popular recipes.

Sharp has been fortunate enough to raise a family near her hometown in Pennsylvania where she, her husband and children live in a beautiful rustic house on an extensive piece of land. Her other passion is taking care of the furry members of her family which include 3 cats, 2 dogs and a potbelly pig named Wilbur.

Watch for more amazing books by Stephanie Sharp coming out in the next few months.

Author's Afterthoughts

I am truly grateful to you for taking the time to read my book. I cherish all of my readers! Thanks ever so much to each of my cherished readers for investing the time to read this book!

With so many options available to you, your choice to buy my book is an honour, so my heartfelt thanks at reading it from beginning to end!

I value your feedback, so please take a moment to submit an honest and open review on Amazon so I can get valuable insight into my readers' opinions and others can benefit from your experience.

Thank you for taking the time to review!

Stephanie Sharp

For announcements about new releases, please

follow my author page on Amazon.com!

(Look for the Follow Bottom under the photo)

You can find that at:

https://www.amazon.com/author/stephanie-sharp

*or Scan **QR-code** below.*

Printed in Great Britain
by Amazon

65004935R00073